Penguin Coloring Book For Adults

A Stress Relief Adult Coloring Book Of 40 Penguin Designs in a Variety of Intricate Patterns

Adult Coloring World

ISBN-13: 978-1523229154
ISBN-10: 1523229152

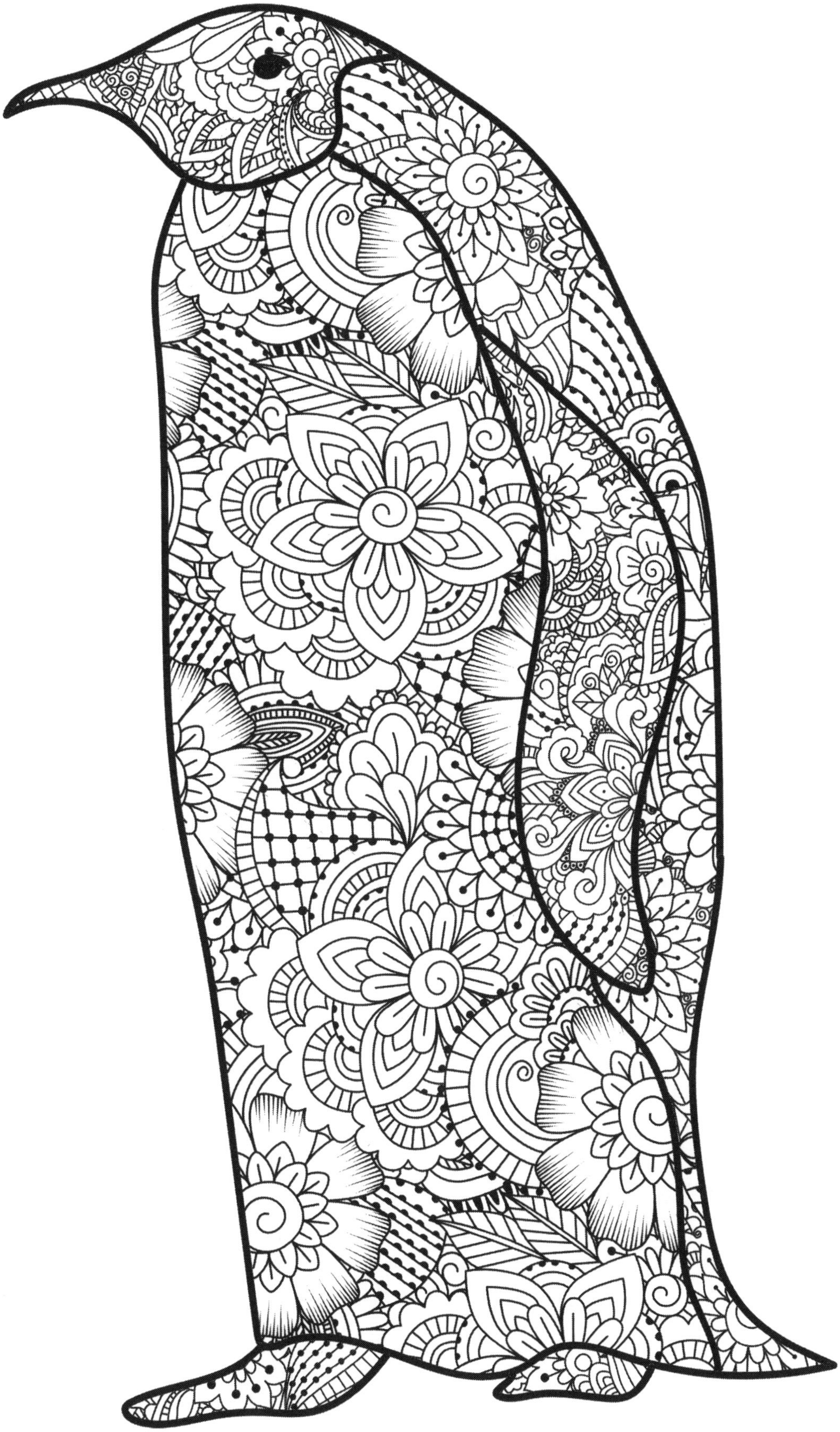

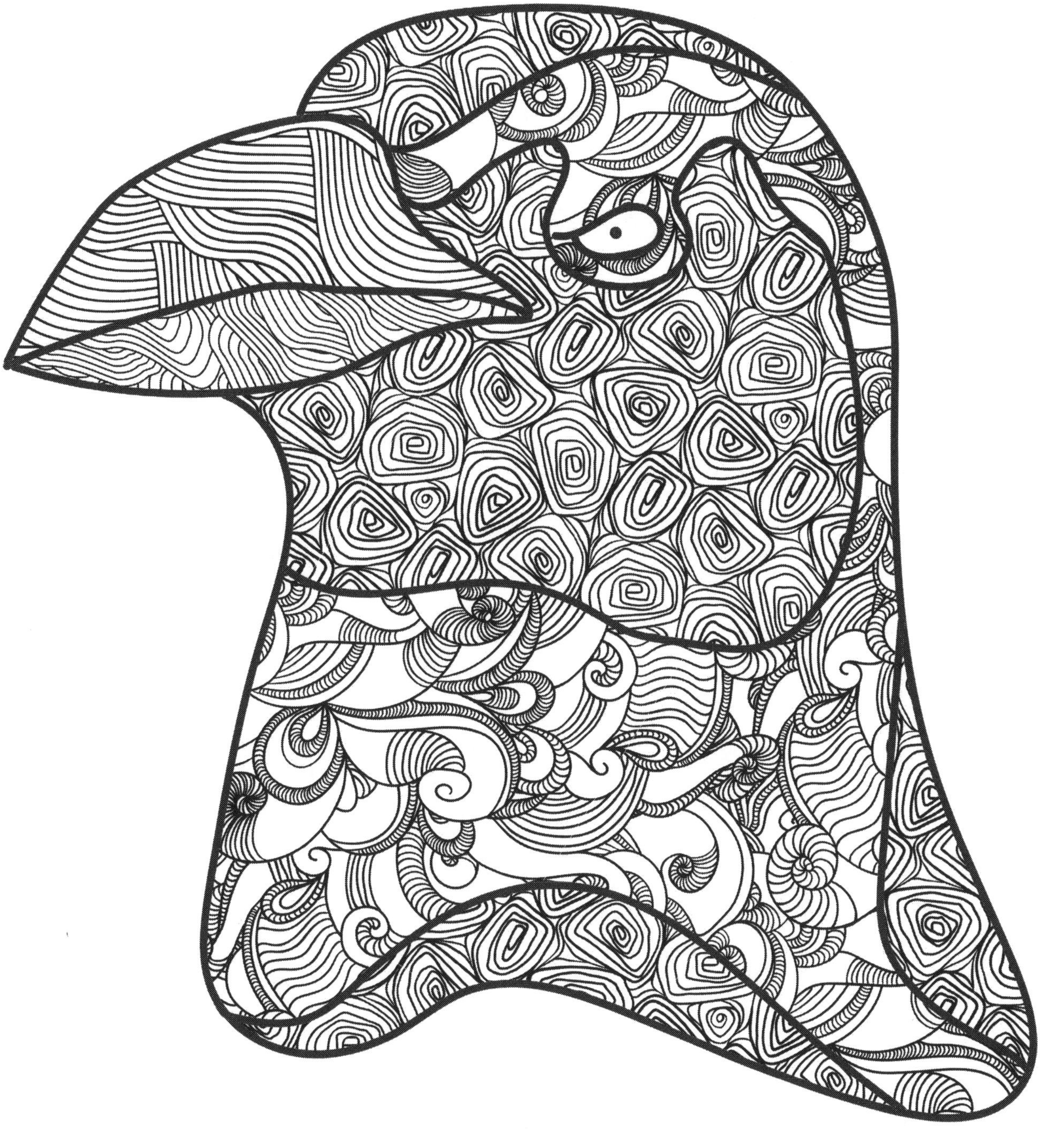

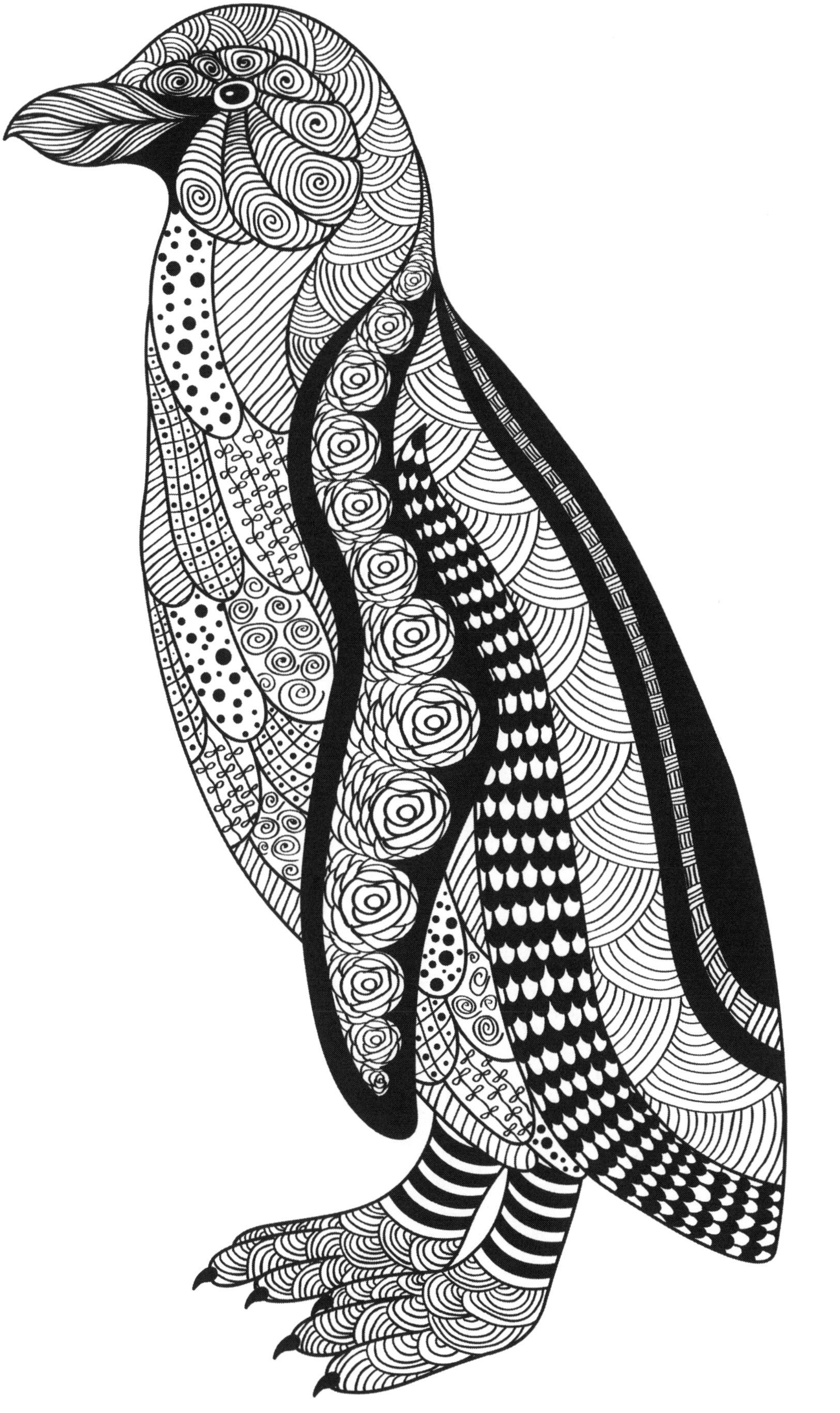

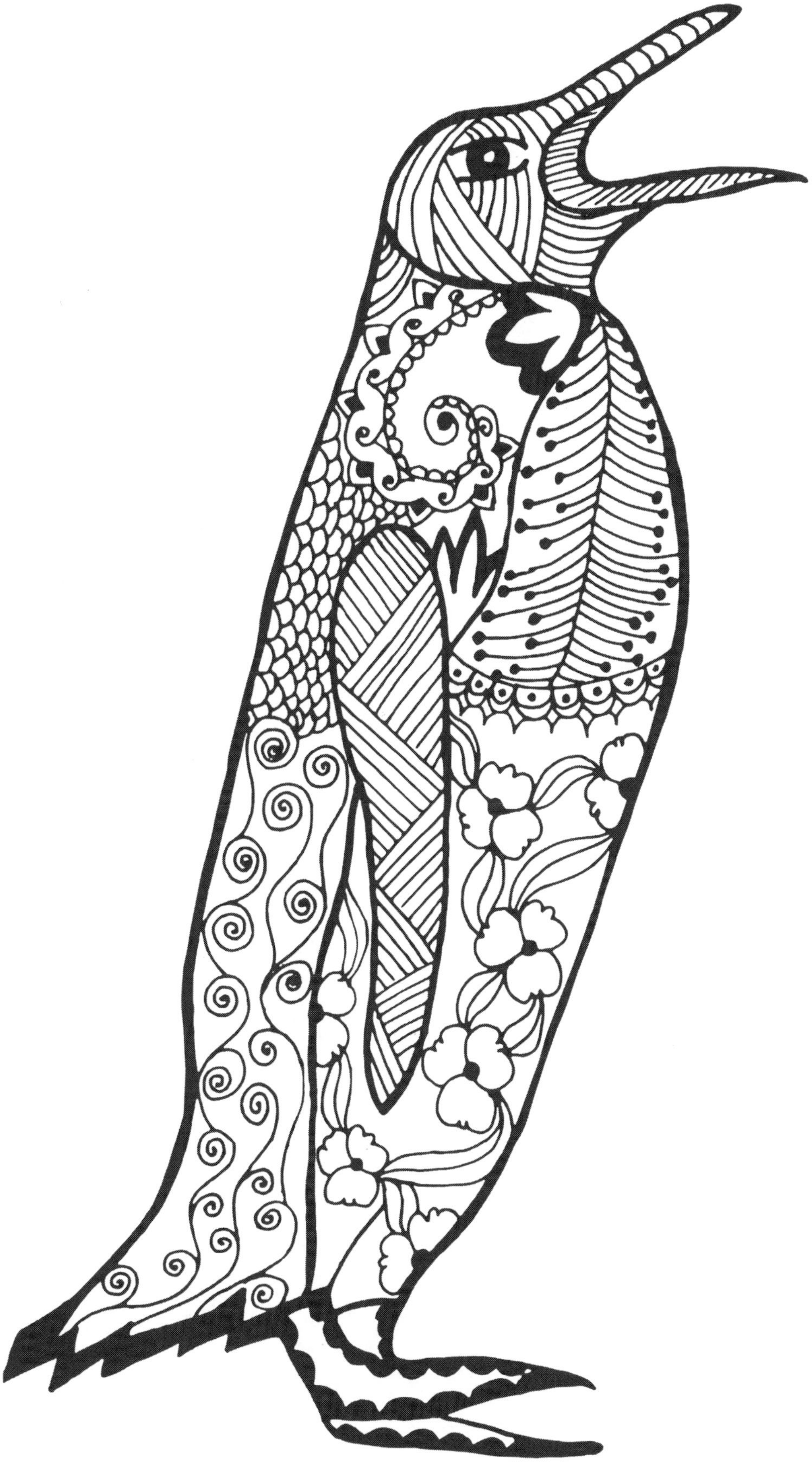

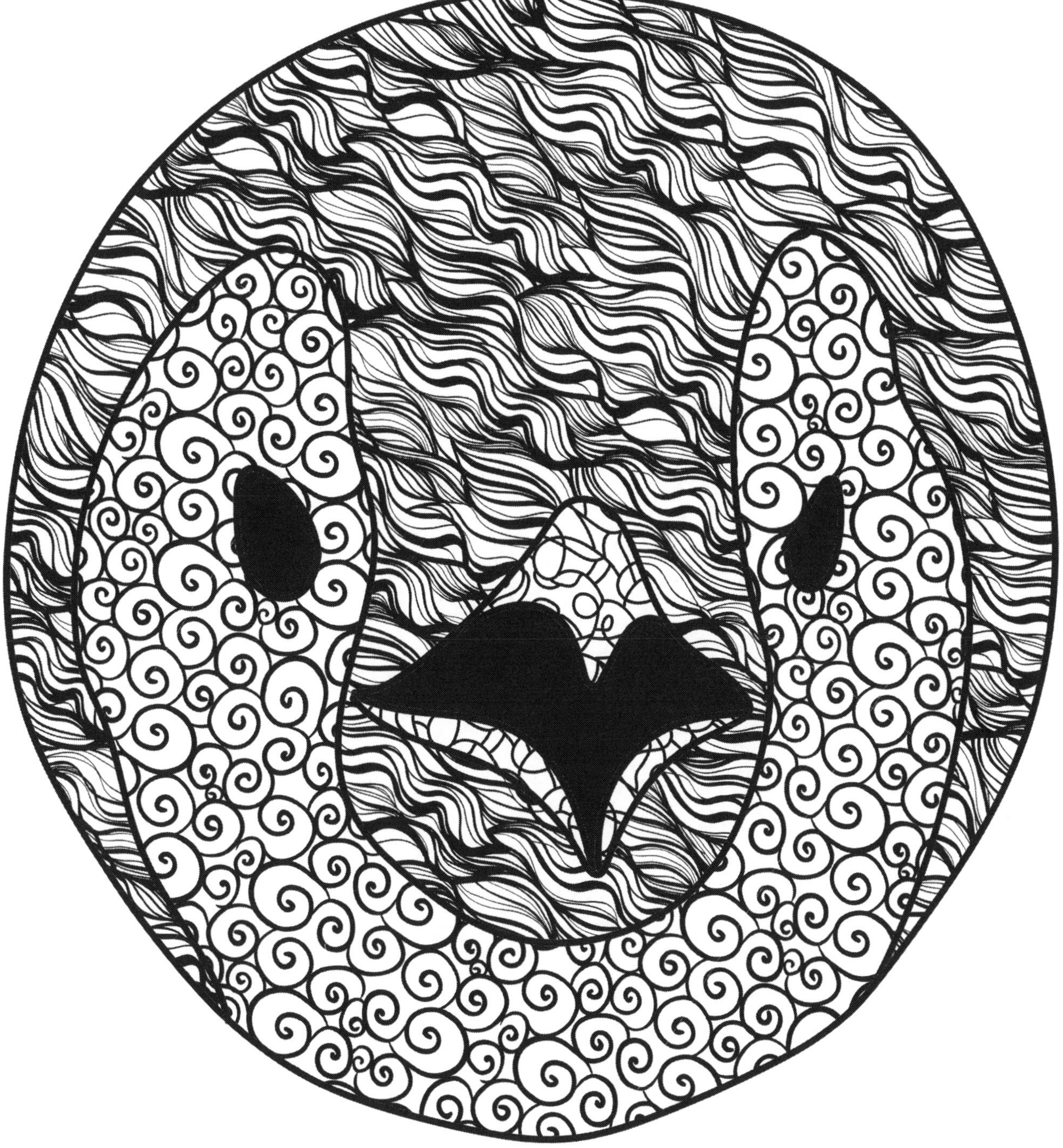

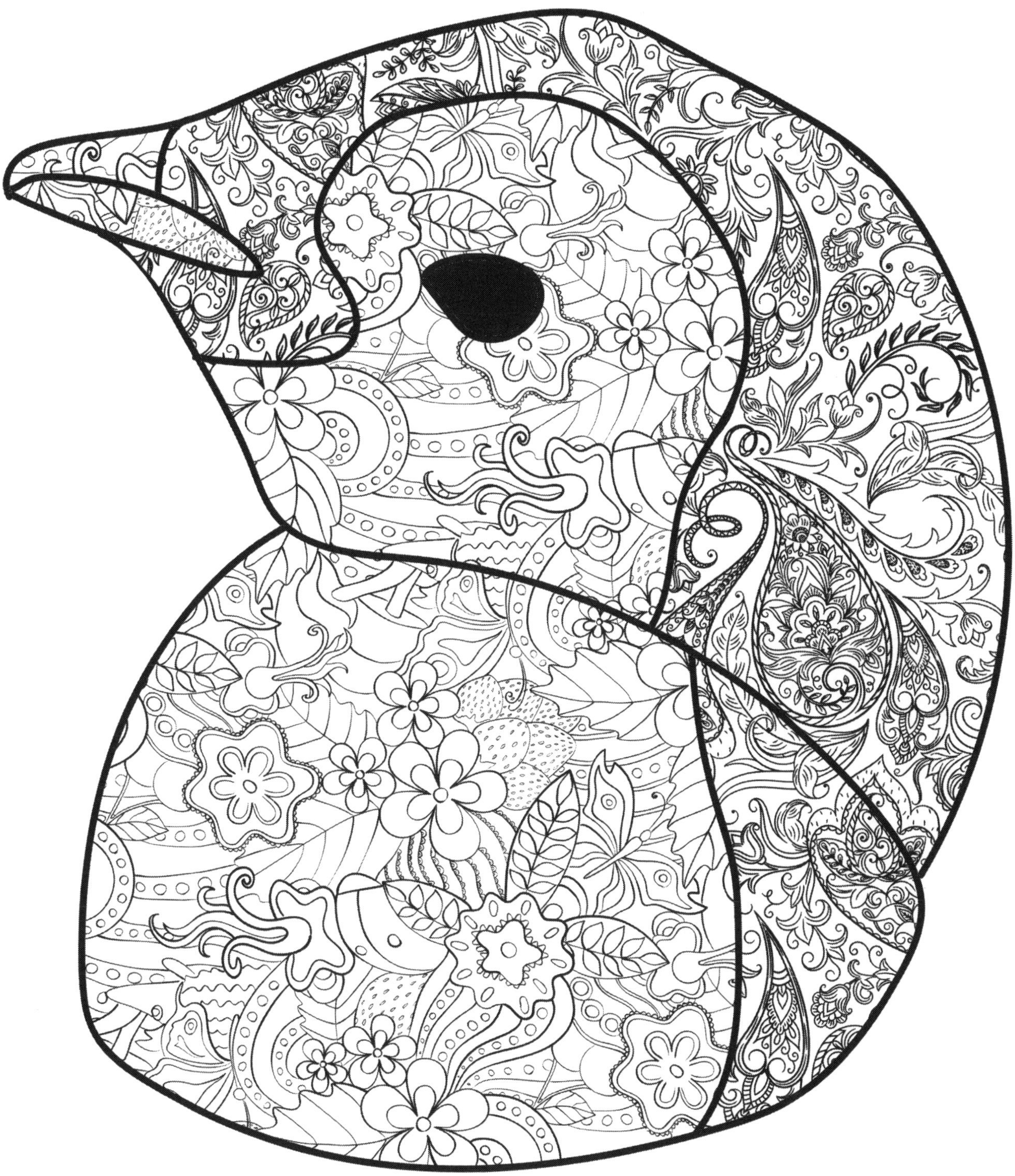

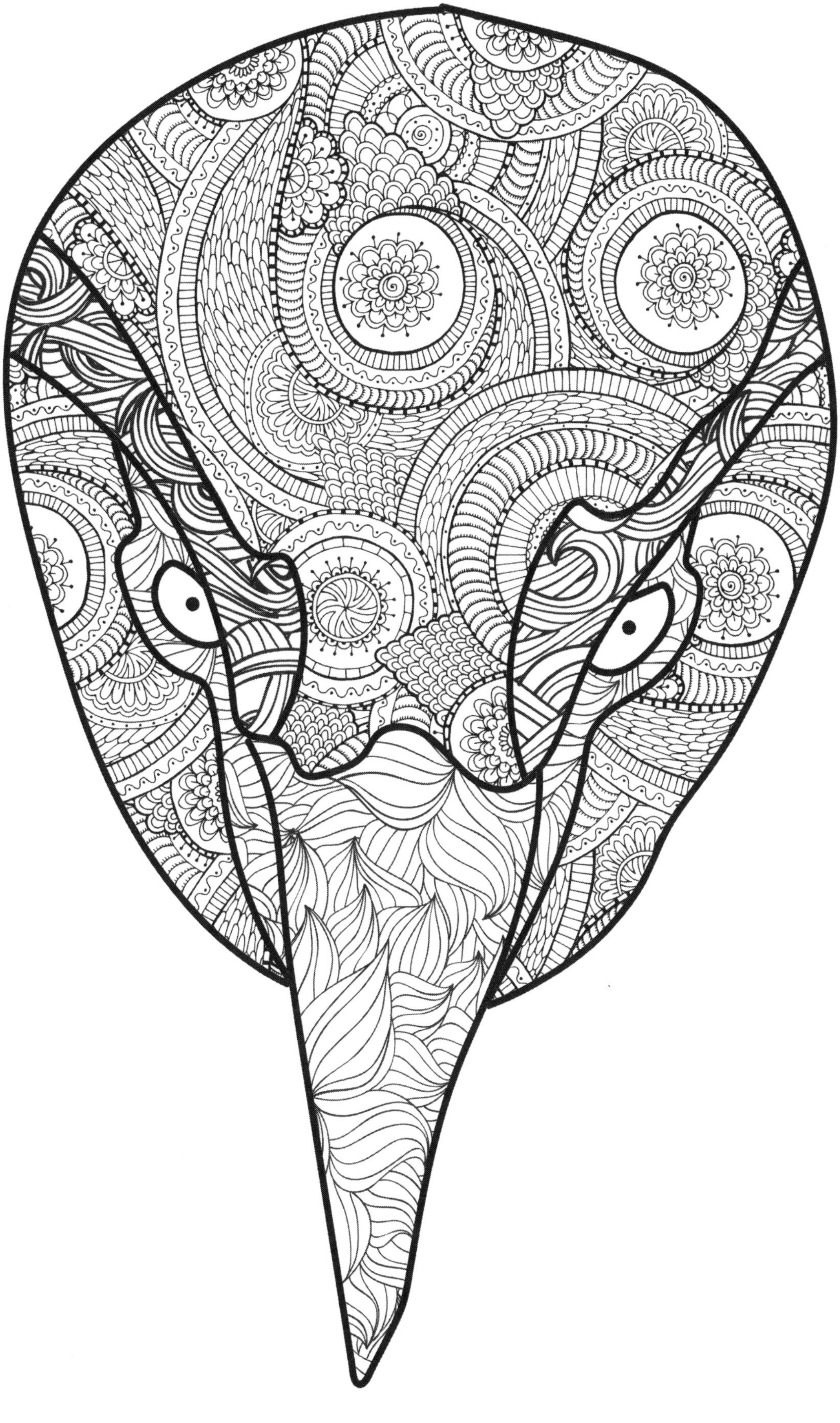

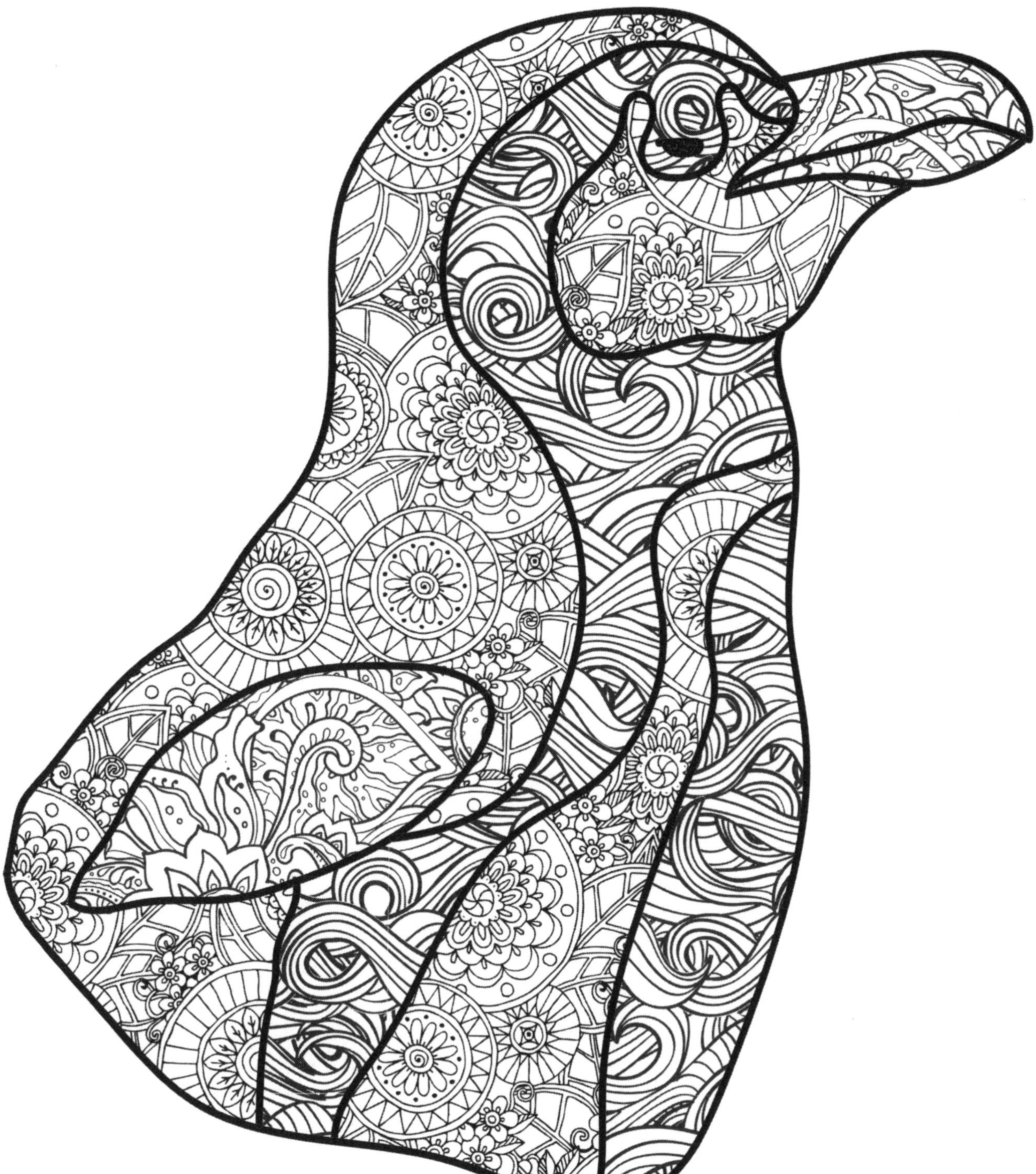

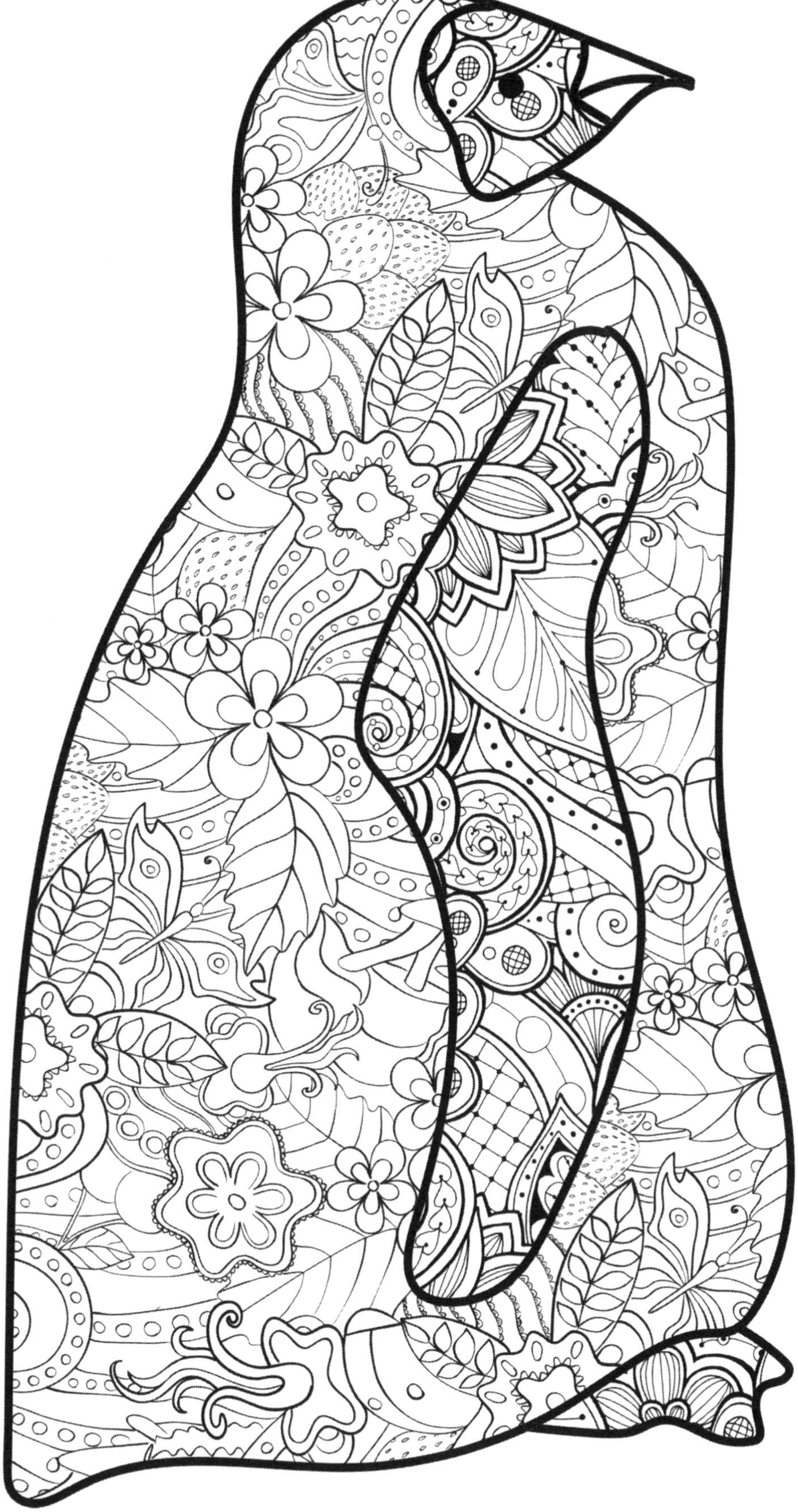

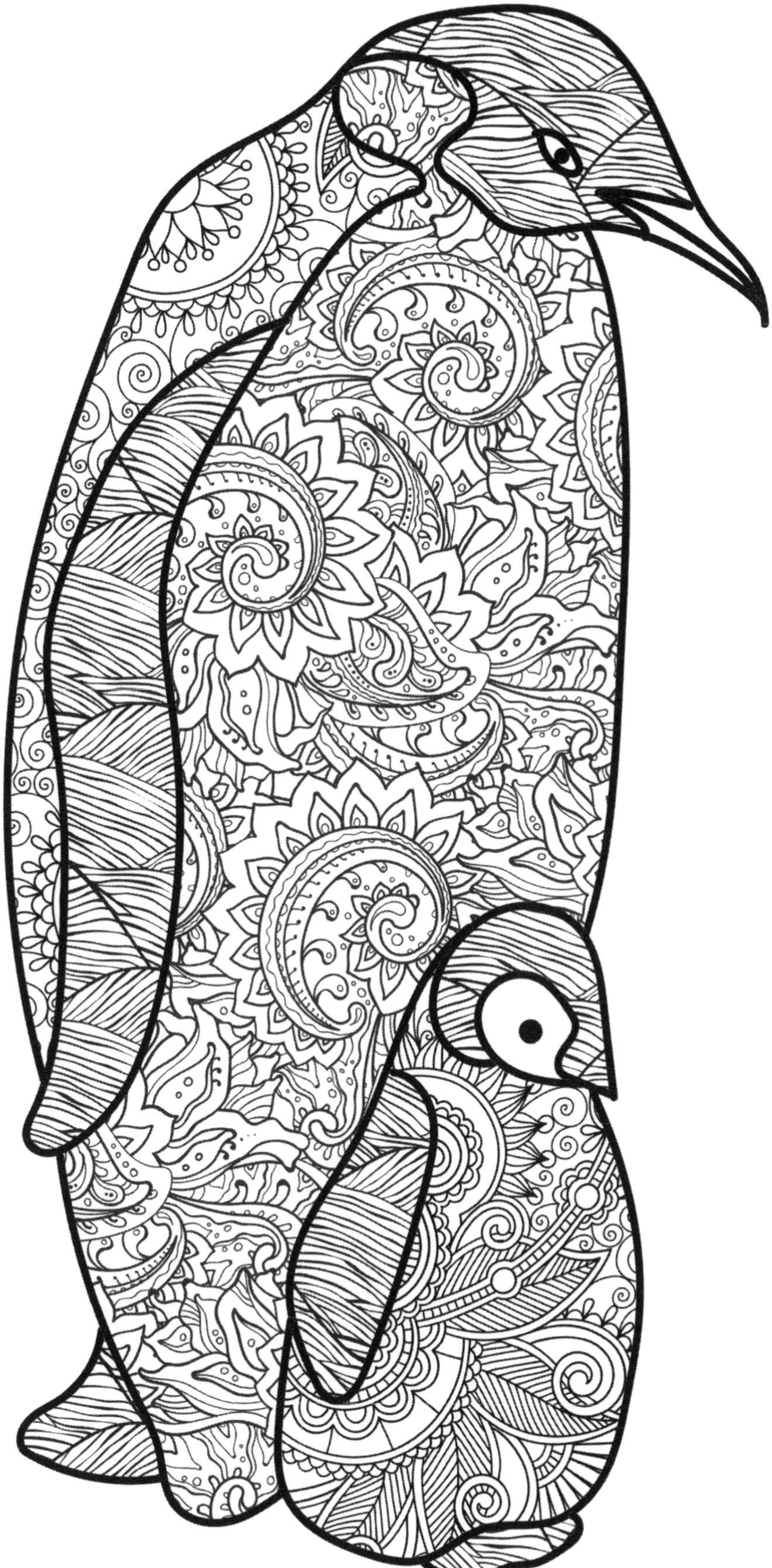

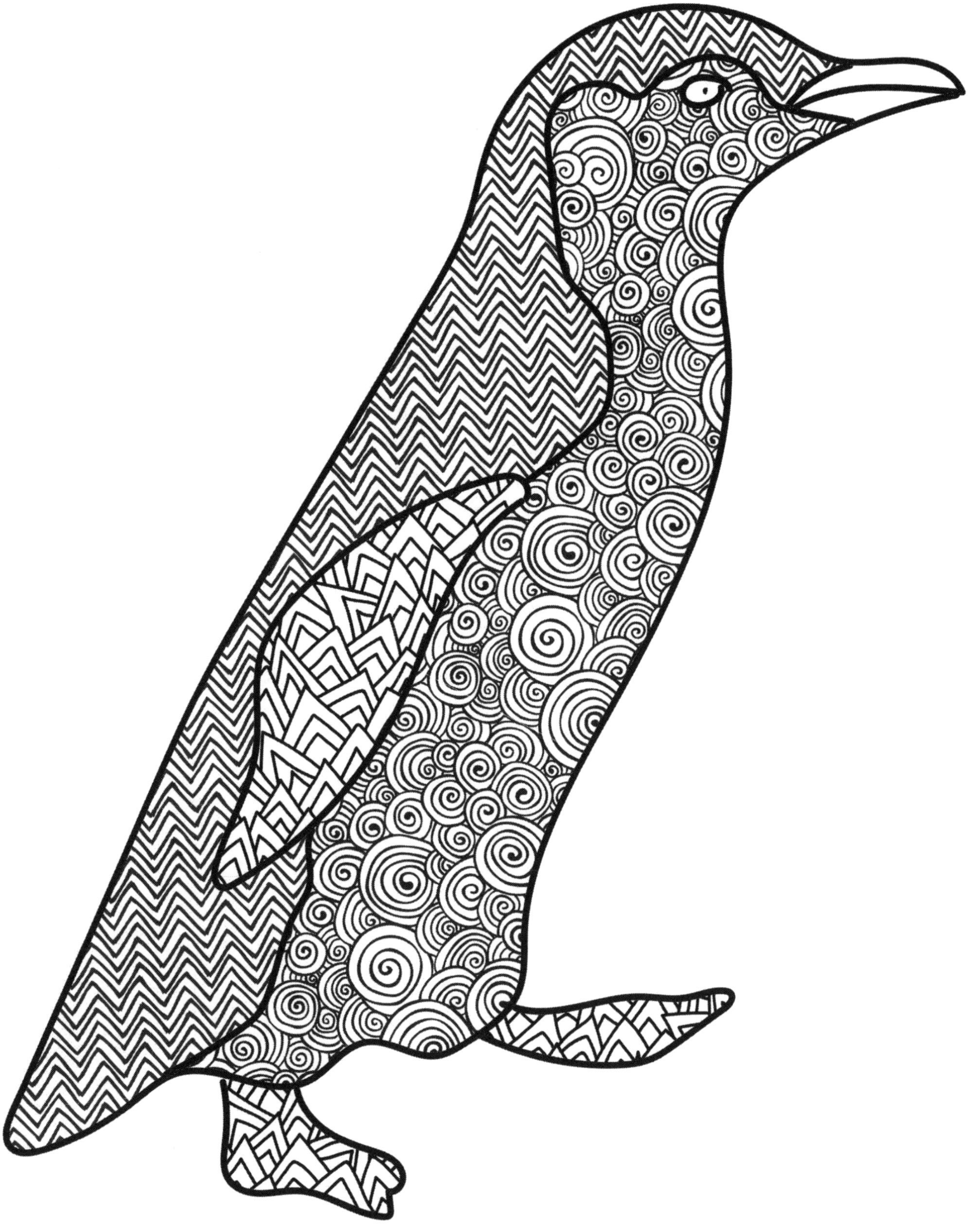

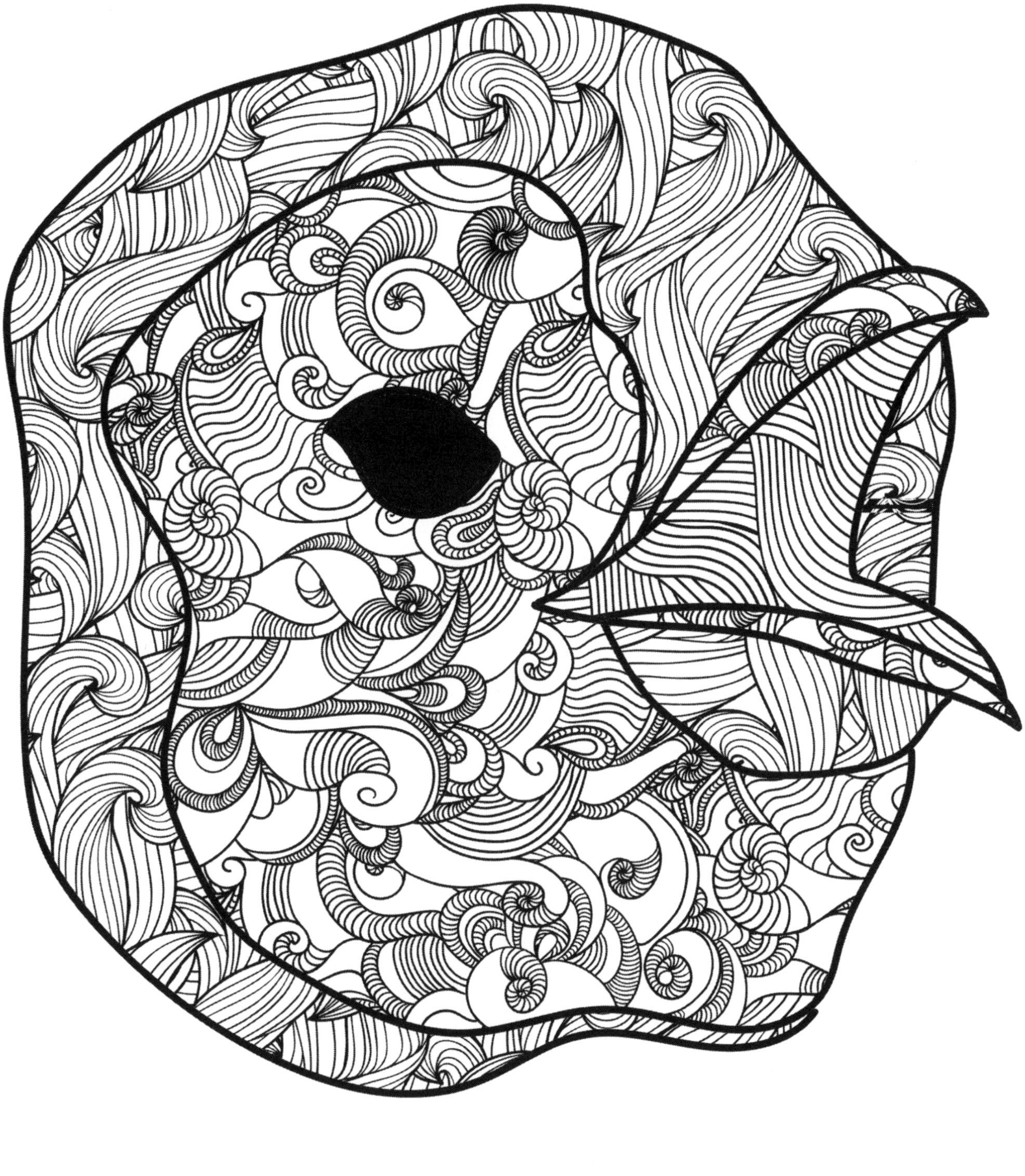

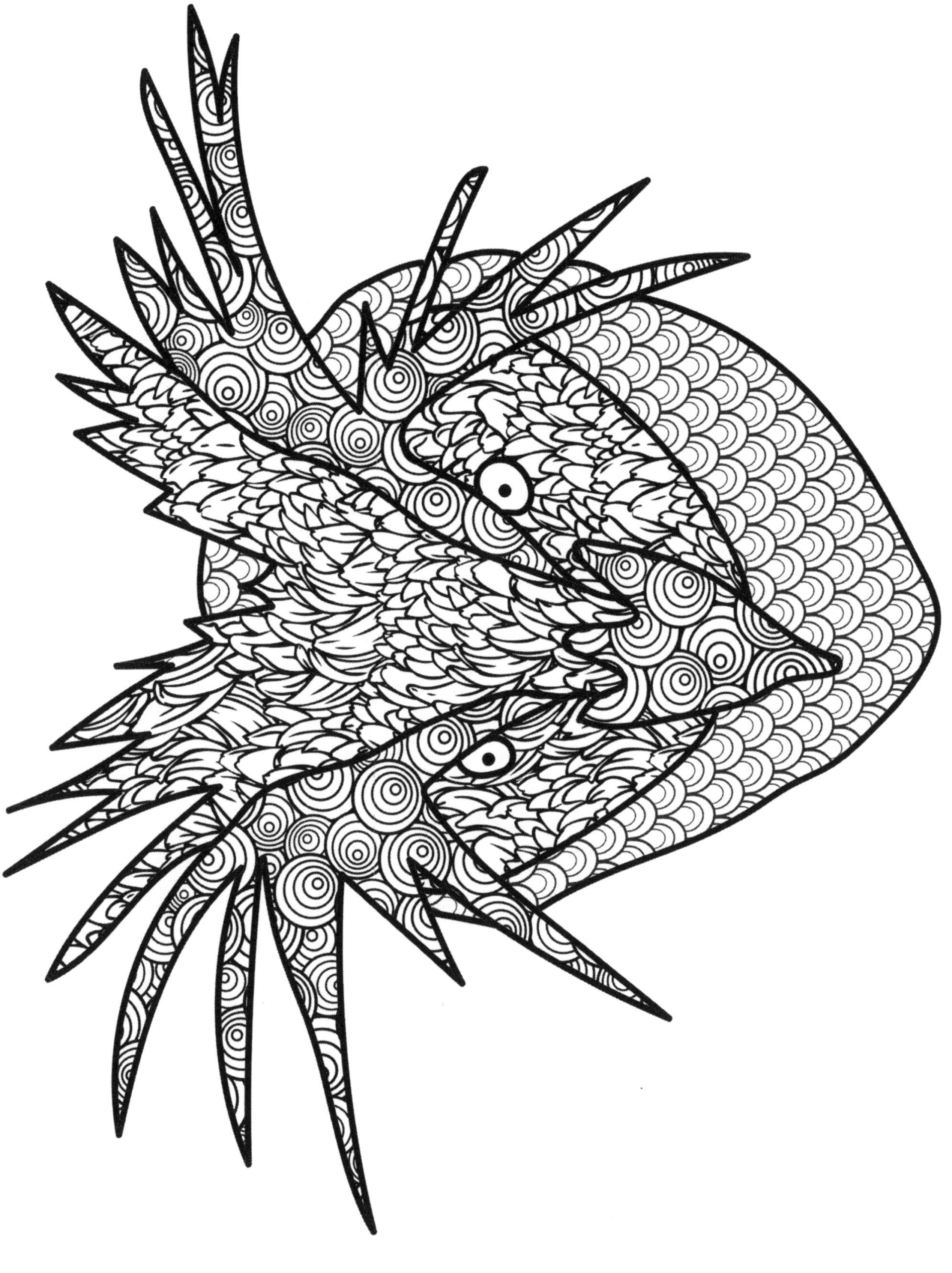

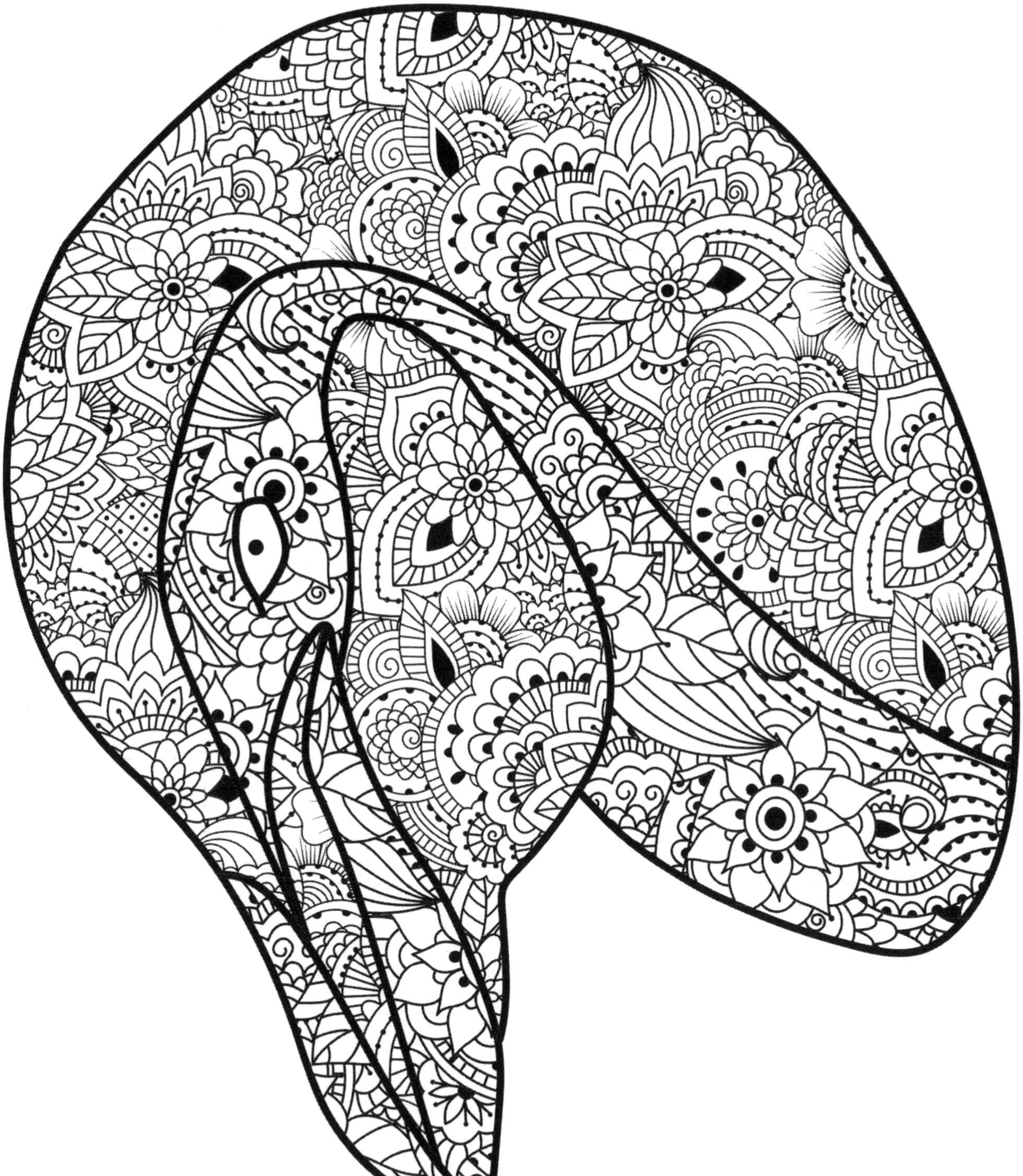

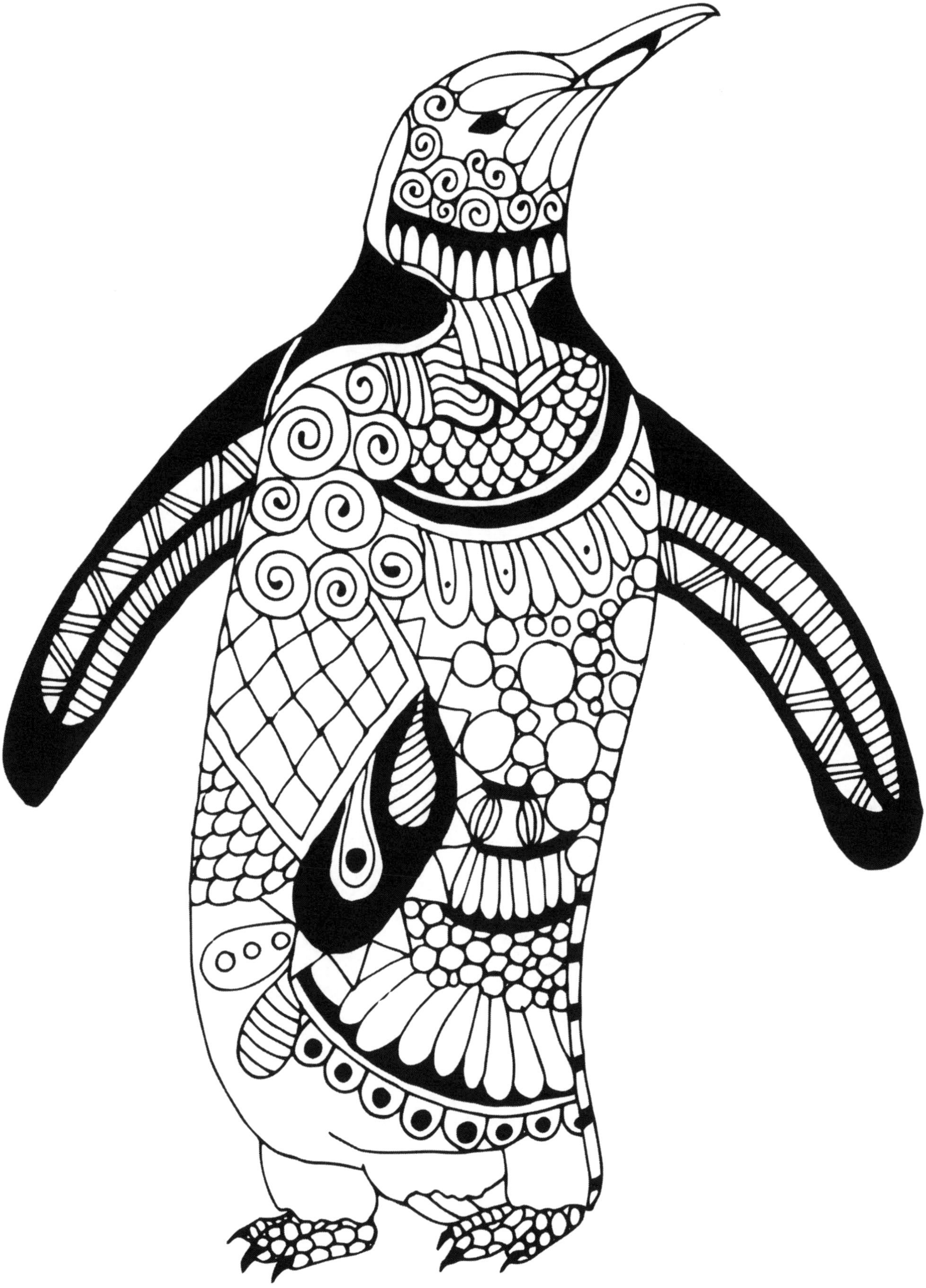

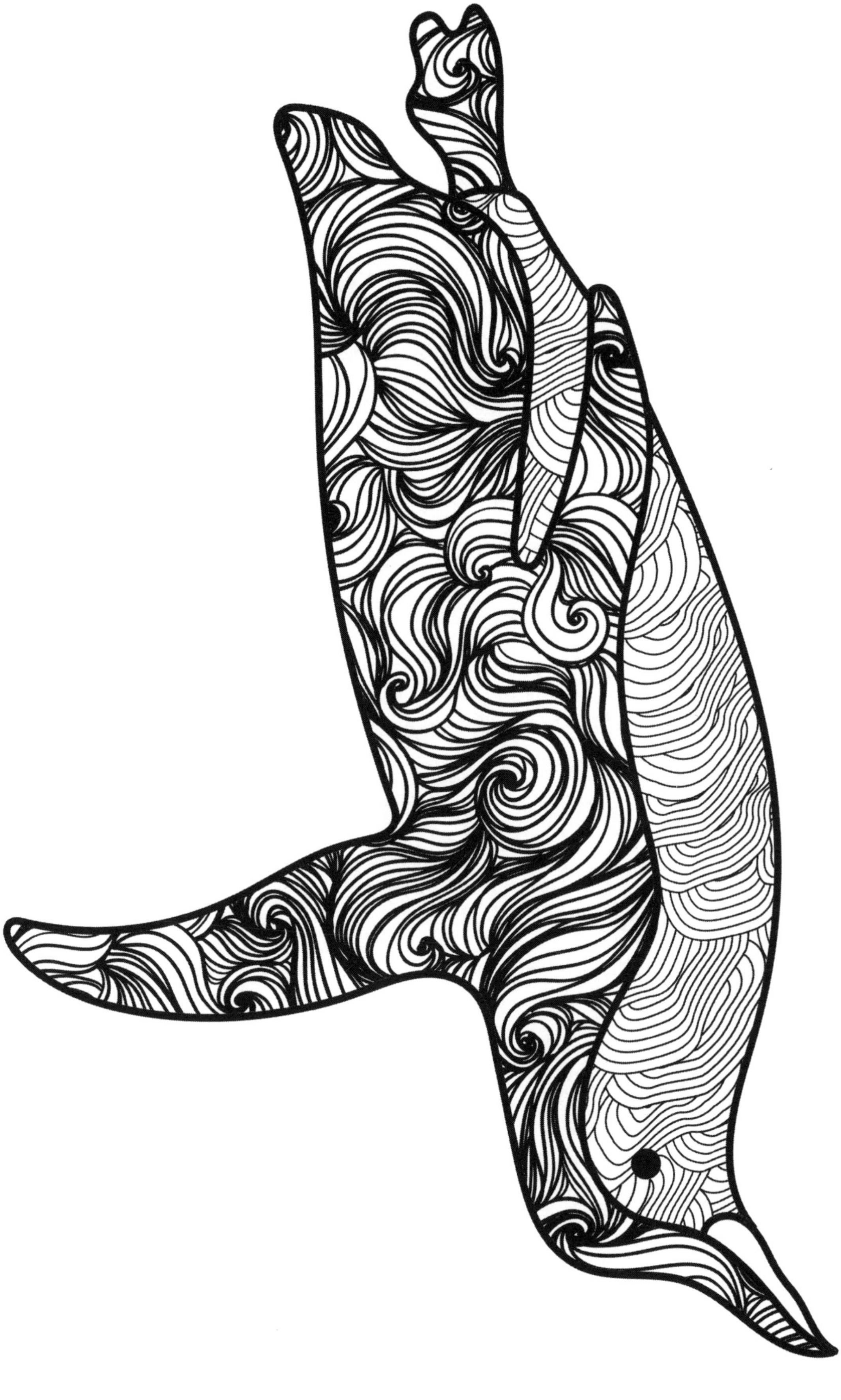

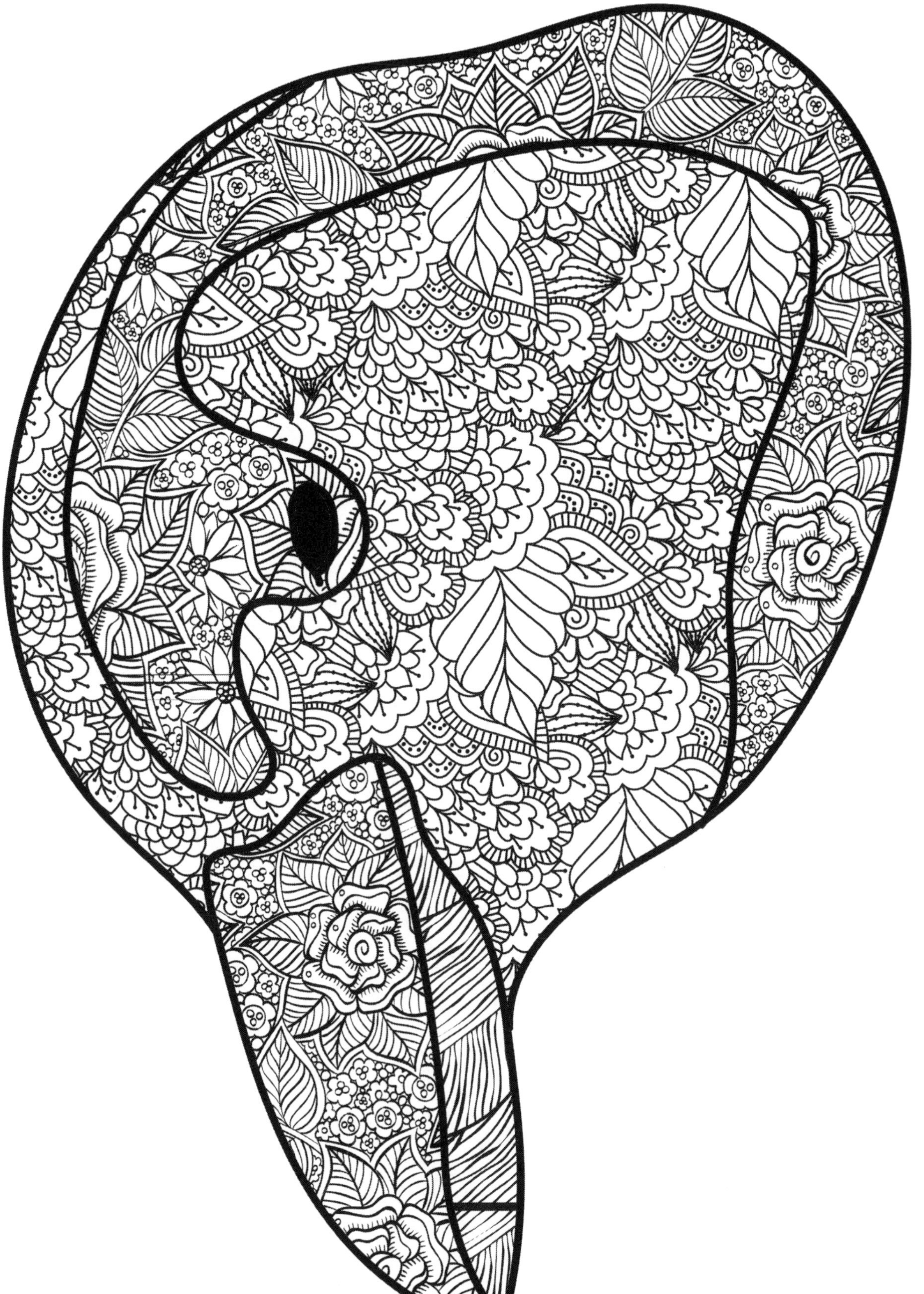

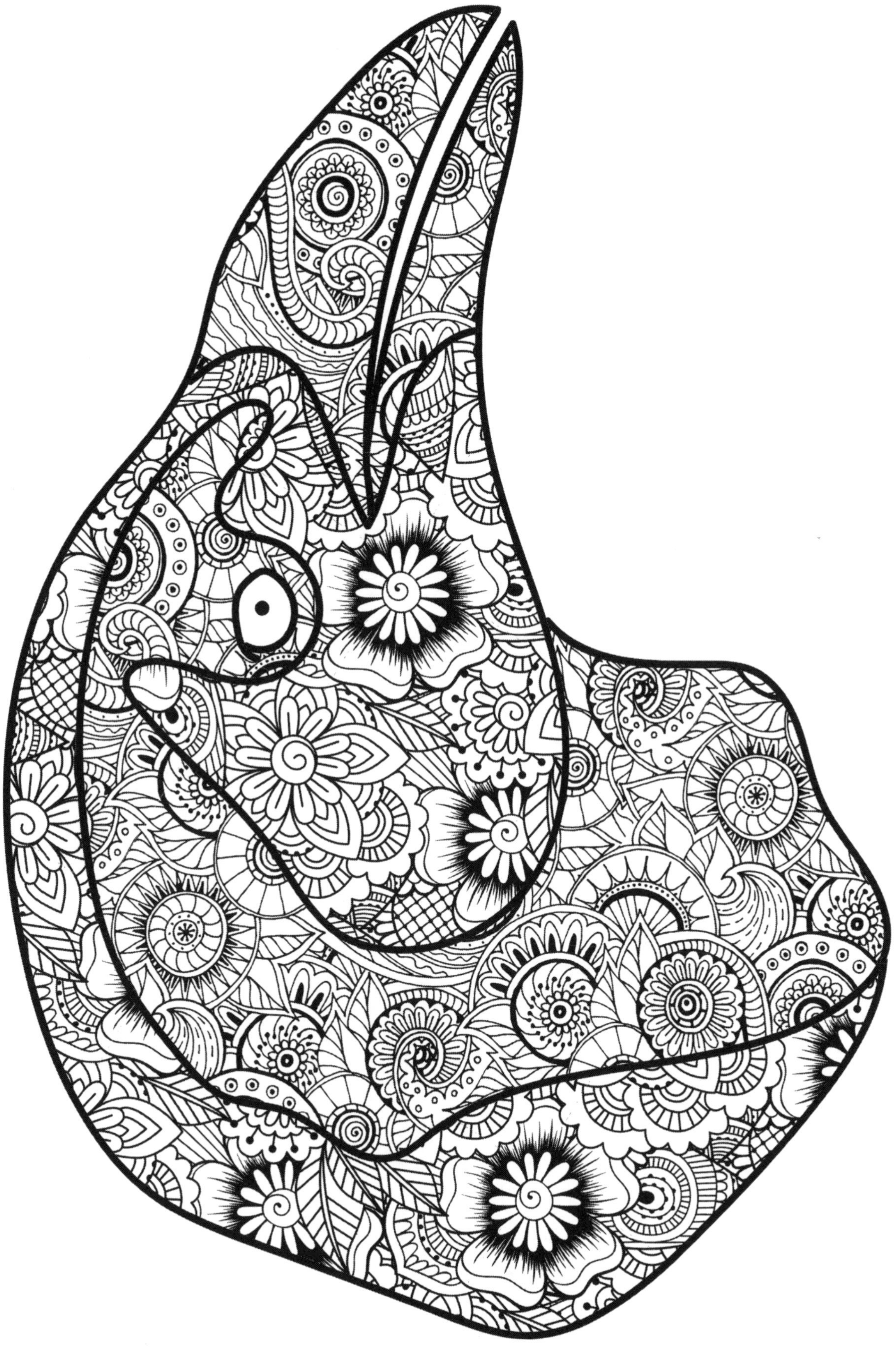

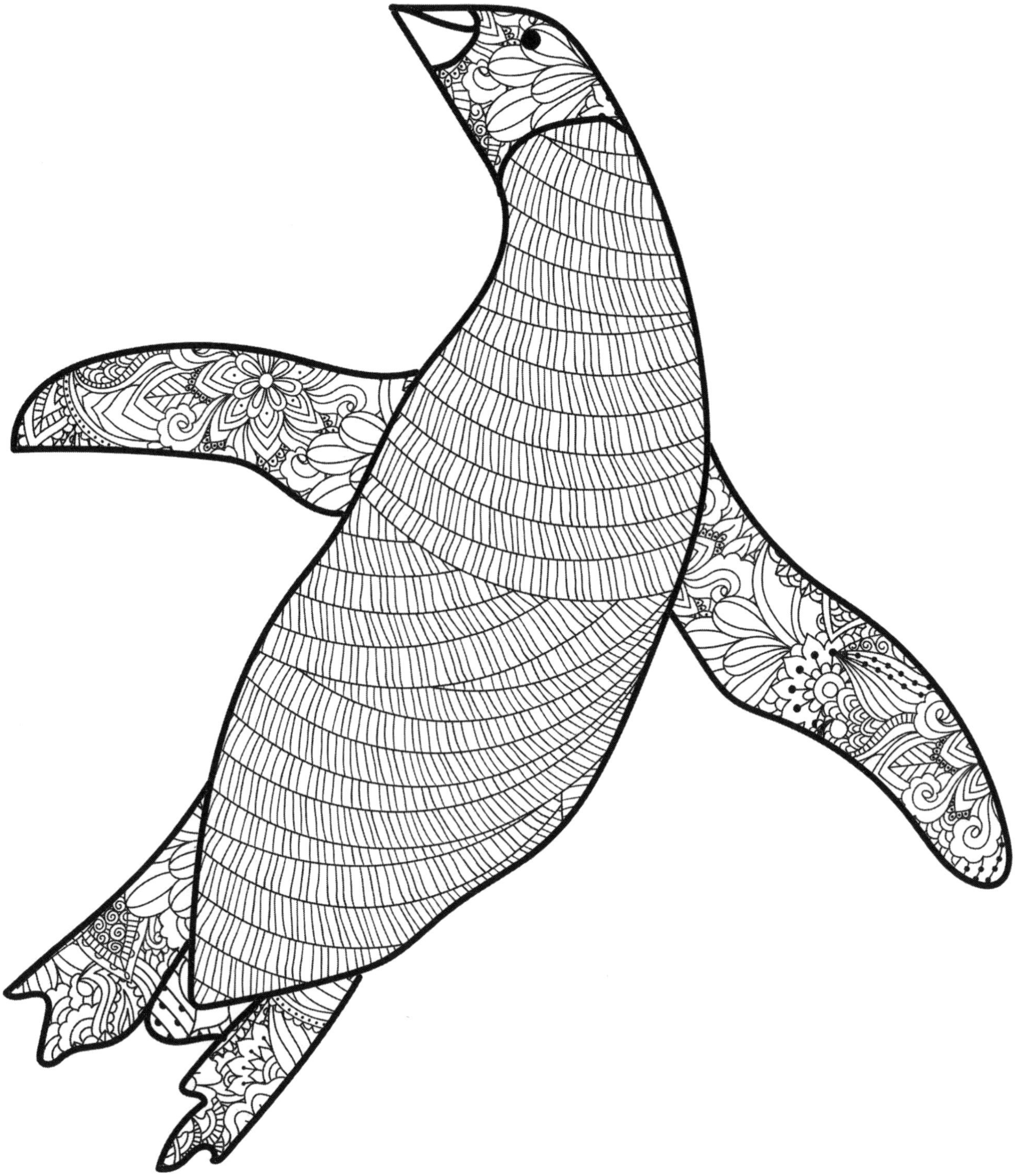

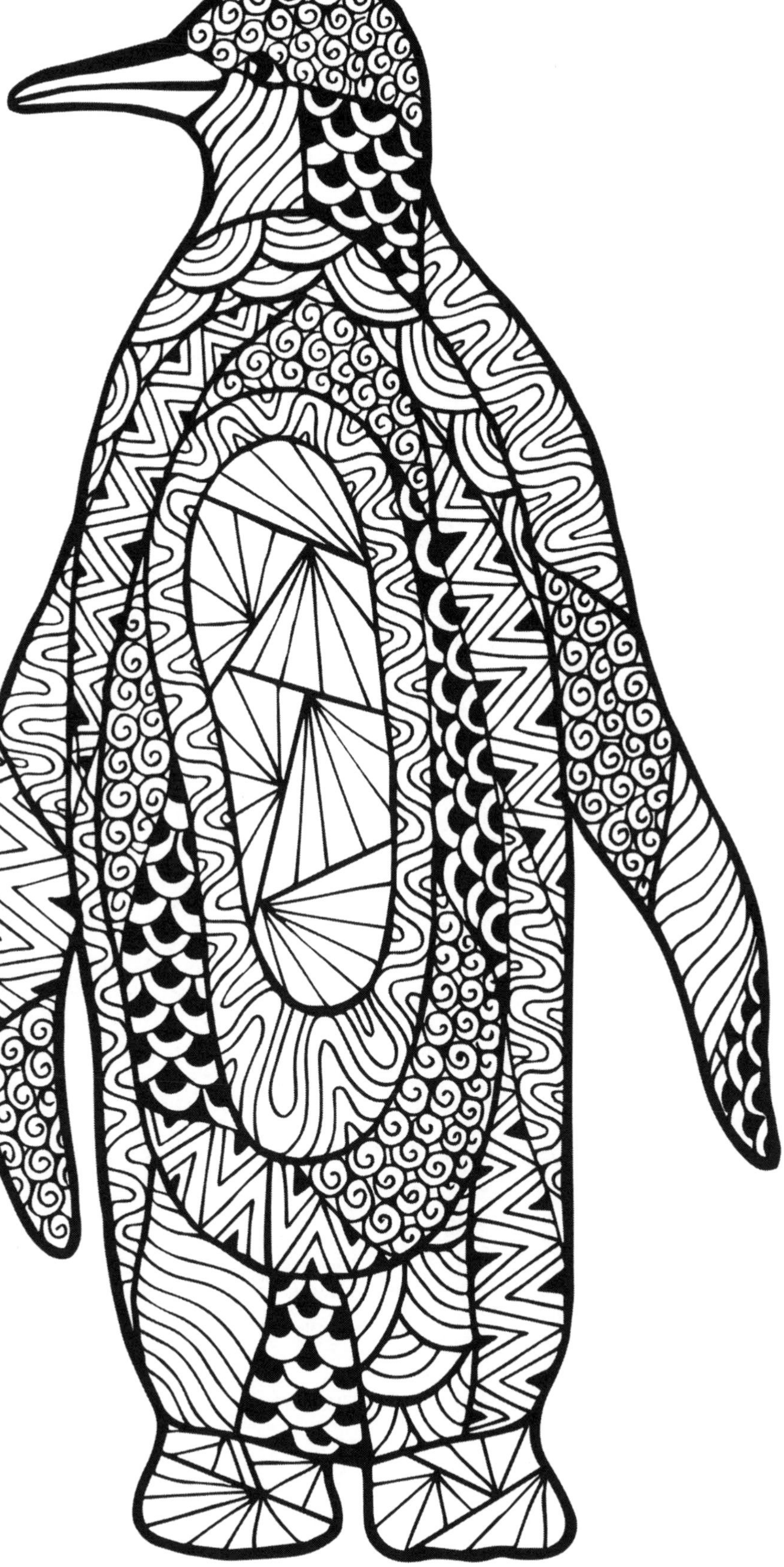

11690648R00046

Made in the USA
Lexington, KY
14 October 2018